A LifeBuilder

C000065180

IMAGES of THE SPIRIT

8 studies
for individuals or groups

Dale & Sandy Larsen

with notes for leaders

Scripture Union is an international Christian charity working with churches in more than 130 countries providing resources to bring the good news about Jesus Christ to children, young people and families – and to encourage them to develop spiritually through the Bible and prayer. As well as coordinating a network of volunteers, staff and associates who run holidays, church-based events and school Christian groups, Scripture Union produces a wide range of publications and supports those who use their resources through training programmes.

Scripture Union, 207-209 Queensway, Bletchley, MK2 2EB, UK.
e-mail: info@scriptureunion.org.uk
www.scriptureunion.org.uk

Scripture Union Australia: Locked Bag 2, Central Coast Business Centre, NSW 2252. www.su.org.au

ISBN 978 1 84427 278 5

First published in the United States by InterVarsity Press.
Published in Great Britain by Scripture Union 2007.

© all editions Dale & Sandy Larsen

Scripture quotations, unless otherwise indicated, are taken from the Holy Bible, New International Version. Copyright © 1973, 1978, 1984 by International Bible Society. Anglicisation copyright © 1979, 1984, 1989. Used by permission of Hodder and Stoughton Limited.

British Library Cataloguing-in-Publication data: a catalogue record for this book is available from the British Library.

Printed in Great Britain by goodmanbaylis, The Trinity Press, Worcester and London.

Contents

Getting the Most Out of
Images of the Spirit

When we think of Jesus Christ, we immediately have a mental picture of a person. His features are heavily influenced by the paintings hung in Sunday school rooms or the pictures in our Bibles, but we think of a person. When we think of God the Father, we fall back even more heavily on artists' conceptions, but we can still imagine a person.

The Holy Spirit is different. When we think of the Holy Spirit, we have trouble coming up with anything like a mental image of a person. Our imagination is likely to run to something more like a vague fuzzy cloud. Or perhaps we think of an invisible impersonal force. No wonder the Holy Spirit is often called "it." While Christians affirm that the Spirit is the third person of the Trinity, we struggle to think of him as a person at all.

The Bible is clear that the Holy Spirit is a person. But how can human beings understand who he is? Scripture helps us by giving us strong word pictures of the Spirit. In this study guide we will look at eight of them.

The eight images in this book are not the only scriptural images of the Spirit. Others occur occasionally in the Bible. To our surprise, some of the most familiar images are the least common in Scripture. The Holy Spirit in the form of a dove, so prevalent in jewelry and in church architecture, appears only once in Scripture, although it comes at a noteworthy occasion—the baptism of Jesus.

As we study each of these scriptural word pictures of the

Holy Spirit, we are interested in more than the beauty of poetic language. We want to focus on *our relationship to the reality behind the image*. We may enjoy the idea that the Spirit flows like life-giving water, but the water does us no good unless we drink it. We may ponder the idea that the Spirit is our Counselor, but his counsel will help us only if we listen and obey. We may be pleased that the Spirit bestows spiritual gifts, but if we do not accept and use his gifts, they will be of no benefit to us or to others. So, in these studies you'll find more than information—you'll find an invitation into the work and life of the Spirit.

At the conclusion of each study you will find three extra features:

- Guidance for prayer. Feel free to use these ideas whether you are studying in a group or individually.
- A "Now or Later" section. This includes suggestions for further study and ways to confirm the lesson and apply it to everyday life.
- A list of hymns based on the scriptural image. Many hymns have been inspired by the rich poetic imagery of the Bible. You may sing one or more of them, or simply read the words. The lists are not exhaustive! You will probably recall other hymns or choruses based on each image.

Suggestions for Individual Study

1. As you begin each study, pray that God will speak to you through his Word.

2. Read the introduction to the study and respond to the personal reflection question or exercise. This is designed to help you focus on God and on the theme of the study.

3. Each study deals with a particular passage—so that you can delve into the author's meaning in that context. Read and reread the passage to be studied. The questions are written using the language of the New International Version, so you may wish to use that version of the Bible. The New Revised Standard Version is also recommended.

4. This is an inductive Bible study, designed to help you discover for yourself what Scripture is saying. The study includes three types of questions. *Observation* questions ask about the basic facts: who, what, when, where and how. *Interpretation* questions delve into the meaning of the passage. *Application* questions help you discover the implications of the text for growing in Christ. These three keys unlock the treasures of Scripture.

Write your answers to the questions in the spaces provided or in a personal journal. Writing can bring clarity and deeper understanding of yourself and of God's Word.

5. It might be good to have a Bible dictionary handy. Use it to look up any unfamiliar words, names or places.

6. Use the prayer suggestion to guide you in thanking God for what you have learned and to pray about the applications that have come to mind.

7. You may want to go on to the suggestion under "Now or Later," or you may want to use that idea for your next study.

Suggestions for Members of a Group Study

1. Come to the study prepared. Follow the suggestions for individual study mentioned above. You will find that careful preparation will greatly enrich your time spent in group discussion.

2. Be willing to participate in the discussion. The leader of your group will not be lecturing. Instead, he or she will be encouraging the members of the group to discuss what they have learned. The leader will be asking the questions that are found in this guide.

3. Stick to the topic being discussed. Your answers should be based on the verses which are the focus of the discussion and not on outside authorities such as commentaries or speakers. These studies focus on a particular passage of Scripture. Only rarely should you refer to other portions of the Bible. This allows for everyone to participate in in-depth study on equal ground.

4. Be sensitive to the other members of the group. Listen attentively when they describe what they have learned. You may be surprised by their insights! Each question assumes a variety of answers. Many questions do not have "right" answers, particularly questions that aim at meaning or application. Instead the questions push us to explore the passage more thoroughly.

When possible, link what you say to the comments of others. Also, be affirming whenever you can. This will encourage some of the more hesitant members of the group to participate.

5. Be careful not to dominate the discussion. We are sometimes so eager to express our thoughts that we leave too little opportunity for others to respond. By all means participate! But allow others to also.

6. Expect God to teach you through the passage being discussed and through the other members of the group. Pray that you will have an enjoyable and profitable time together, but also that as a result of the study you will find ways that you can take action individually and/or as a group.

7. Remember that anything said in the group is considered confidential and should not be discussed outside the group unless specific permission is given to do so.

8. If you are the group leader, you will find additional suggestions at the back of the guide.

1

Wind/Breath

Ezekiel 37:1-14

In the days of the great sailing ships, wind opened up the possibility of trade around the globe. Windmills pump water and generate electricity. At its wildest, at hurricane or tornado force, wind flips cars and demolishes buildings. Wind at tamer speeds keeps kites aloft on a brisk March day.

Breath, though less forceful than wind, is more of a life-and-death matter. A person can live for weeks without food, days without water, but only minutes without breath.

The same Hebrew word can be translated *wind, breath* or *spirit*. All three are powerful but invisible. No one can see them, but everyone can see their effects.

GROUP DISCUSSION. When has wind felt especially good to you?

PERSONAL REFLECTION. Think of someone you would describe as "a breath of fresh air." Why would you describe the person in that way?

Ezekiel was God's prophet to the exiled Jewish community in Babylon in the 6th century B.C. The Babylonian king Nebuchadnezzar had broken down the walls of Jerusalem, burned the temple and deported thousands of Jews as captives. While Ezekiel pronounced God's judgment on Israel, he also proclaimed messages of hope. *Read Ezekiel 37:1-14.*

1. At what points does *breath* play an important role in this passage?

2. How does Ezekiel wind up in this unidentified valley (v. 1)?

3. Imagine that, along with Ezekiel, you find yourself in the valley of dry bones (vv. 1-2). How are you affected by what you see?

4. What are God's intentions in the valley of dry bones (vv. 3-6)?

5. You are still a spectator in the valley when Ezekiel obeys God's command to prophesy to the bones. What do you see, hear and feel (vv. 7-8)?

6. God's work in the valley of dry bones was still incomplete. How does God, through Ezekiel, finish restoring the multitude to life (vv. 8-10)?

7. How does God explain the significance of what has just happened (vv. 11-14)?

8. What difference would you expect the Spirit of God to make in the renewal of exiled Israel (v. 14)?

9. While Ezekiel's vision was for the Jews exiled to Babylon, many people have found hope in his vision of a dead multitude brought to life. Identify your own "valley of dry bones," an area or areas of your life where you have echoed Israel's hopelessness in verse 11.

As you consider that area (or areas), what invitation from God do you find in this passage?

10. How might you be trying to enliven yourself through your own efforts or schemes?

11. How will you remind yourself this week to let go of your own efforts and let the Spirit renew you?

Ask the Holy Spirit to breathe life into places where you feel spiritually weak or even lifeless. Pray that the Spirit will breathe life into others for whom you are concerned.

Now or Later

- Draw your own personal "valley of dry bones." Label individual bones with situations or areas of life in which you feel hopeless. Draw a second picture in which the Holy Spirit reconnects the bones and gives them life. Use the pictures to inspire your continued prayers about those situations.
- Study John 3:1-15, in which Jesus talks with Nicodemus about being born of the Spirit.

Suggested hymns to read or sing
Breathe on Me, Breath of God
O Breath of Life, Come Sweeping Through Us

2

Water

There are Christian missions that concentrate on only one task: drilling wells. People who do not have a reliable source of water must live on the edge of survival. If a village's source of water dries up, the people must walk, perhaps for hours, to get daily water; eventually the entire village may disperse. With a reliable source of water, people can live settled lives, grow crops, tend animals and look toward the future. Water is life. Water is hope.

GROUP DISCUSSION. Look closely at a glass or pitcher of water. Take three minutes to name all the things that water makes possible.

PERSONAL REFLECTION. What is the thirstiest you have ever been? What was it like to finally get water?

Fetching water was a daily task for people in Jesus' time. As he traveled from Judea to Galilee, Jesus wearily sat down by a well. *Read John 4:7-14.*

---

1. Compare and contrast what Jesus and the Samaritan woman mean by *water.*

---

2. Suppose you hear Jesus' words in verses 10, 13-14. What questions arise in your mind?

---

3. At what point in the discussion does the meaning of *water* shift from physical to spiritual (vv. 7-10)?

---

4. The woman is at first skeptical of Jesus' promise (vv. 11-12). How does he answer her doubts with hope (vv. 13-14)?

---

5. How would you define spiritual thirst?

---

6. What are some of the unsatisfactory ways in which people try to quench their spiritual thirst?

7. The water that Jesus offers has unusual features. What are they (v. 14)?

Later in his ministry, when he was in Jerusalem for the Feast of Tabernacles, Jesus identified *living water* more specifically. *Read John 7:37-39.*

8. What would you think about a person who stood up in public and made such an audacious invitation as this (v. 37)?

9. Why do you think Jesus spoke with "a loud voice" (v. 37)?

10. What qualities will characterize those who believe in Christ (vv. 38-39)?

11. When have you sensed the Holy Spirit flowing from another person to bless you?

12. How have others been refreshed by the Spirit flowing through you?

13. In what ways do you still long for the Holy Spirit to flow more freely in your life?

Acknowledge your thirst to God, and ask his Spirit to satisfy you. Pray that the outflowing of the Spirit in your life will also reach others who are thirsty.

Now or Later

- Study Isaiah 44:1-4, in which the Lord compares the pouring out of his Spirit with the pouring of water on thirsty ground.
- Study Ezekiel 47:1-12, Ezekiel's vision of a great river flowing from the temple of God.

Suggested hymns to read or sing
Joys Are Flowing Like a River
Fill My Cup, Lord
I Heard the Voice of Jesus Say
Like a River Glorious

3

Fire

On Sunday evening October 8, 1871, a fire began in the Chicago barn of the O'Learys. By the time it died out on Tuesday morning, it had burned through over three square miles of Chicago. One hundred thousand people were left homeless.

Fire can cook our food, warm us, comfort us, enchant us—but it is not a docile servant. Fire has a life of its own, and we must respect its power.

GROUP DISCUSSION. When have you most appreciated and been thankful for fire?

PERSONAL REFLECTION. Which of these fires raises the most positive feelings for you, and why: a fireplace; a campfire; a bonfire; a wood stove; a candelabra?

Fire is an apt metaphor for the work of the Holy Spirit. John the Baptist announced, of the coming Christ, "He will baptize you with the Holy Spirit and with fire" (Luke 3:16). After Jesus ascended to heaven, his followers gathered regularly to pray and to wait for the gift God had promised (Acts 1:4-5). *Read Acts 2:1-4.*

---

1. If you had been present in that room, what conflicting emotions might you feel as you watch everything unfold?

Which emotion do you think would have overridden the others?

---

2. What evidence can you find that the tongues of fire are not natural flames (vv. 2-3)?

---

3. How does the fire symbolize what is about to happen (vv. 3-4)?

The disciples' experience of the Holy Spirit is so dramatic that some bystanders accuse them of drunkenness. Peter defends them against the charge and then explains that the scene is the fulfillment of prophecy. *Read Acts 2:14-18.*

4. Various groups of people are identified in Joel's prophecy that Peter quotes. What do you conclude from the variety of people who are included in God's promise of the Spirit?

5. What are the promised results of the Spirit's coming?

6. Consider some of the benefits of fire. How does each benefit correspond to the work of the Holy Spirit in a believer's life?

Light:

Heat:

Purifying:

7. What other effects of fire correspond to the work of the Spirit?

8. How has the fire of the Holy Spirit worked in your life?

---

9. Where do you specifically need the light of the Holy Spirit?

---

10. In what areas of your life do you feel coldness where you need the fire of the Spirit?

---

11. Where does your life need the Spirit's purifying work?

Thank God that the fire of his Spirit has never gone out. Ask him to renew your spirit so others see and feel the reality of Christ in you.

Now or Later

- Plan a service of symbolically burning your sins, regrets and unhealthy habits. Gather around a fire, such as a bonfire, fireplace or wood-burning stove. On scraps of paper, write what you want the Lord to burn away in your life. Commit each piece of paper to the flames as you pray individually or together.

- In Acts 2:16-21, Peter identified what happened at Pentecost as a fulfillment of the prophecy of Joel. Study Joel 2:28-32.

Suggested hymns to read or sing
Come, Holy Spirit, Heart's Desire
Lord God, the Holy Ghost
Thou Whose Purpose Is to Kindle
Come, Holy Ghost, Our Souls Inspire
Holy Ghost, with Light Divine

4

Pledge

When I was given power of attorney for my mother, I became responsible for eighty acres of Illinois farmland. For generations a series of farmers had worked the land for our family. None of the farming arrangements had ever been in writing.

Then our current farmer told me he wanted to cut back, and I had to find a new farmer. This time I wanted a written contract. The new farmer was offended, but I insisted. We signed a contract in which both of us promised to fulfill certain responsibilities. Both our signatures were affixed with the seal of a notary public. The notary's seal was a guarantee that we had indeed made those pledges to one another. The contract was literally *signed, sealed and delivered.*

In our salvation, all the promises are made by God, and he *signs, seals and delivers* them himself. The Holy Spirit is the seal of God's pledge that he will keep his promises.

GROUP DISCUSSION. When have you accepted someone's verbal pledge that work would be done? How did you know that the person was trustworthy? Or when have you had a good experience with a guarantee? When have you had a bad experience with a guarantee? What made the difference?

PERSONAL REFLECTION. On what basis would you accept a down payment for something you want to sell? How do you decide whether the one making the down payment will come through with the balance due?

The apostle Paul wrote to Christian believers in Ephesus, a cosmopolitan city dominated by pagan worship. Paul had spent over two years there, a time marked by extraordinary miracles, public repentance by sorcerers and a near riot by devotees of the goddess Artemis (Acts 19). *Read Ephesians 1:1-14.* Although this study focuses on verses 11-14, it is helpful to read Paul's words leading up to that passage as well.

---

1. In one or two phrases, according to this passage, what does God promise to those who are in Christ?

---

2. Which of the blessings of Christ in verses 3-10 do you most long for, and why?

---

3. What doubts about God might arise in the minds of the Christians in Ephesus who are surrounded by pagan culture?

4. What doubts plague believers today?

5. What are God's gracious intentions for believers (vv. 11-12)?

6. How does the Holy Spirit set apart believers as different from other people (vv. 13-14)?

7. What is the guarantee, which the Spirit makes sure (vv. 13-14)?

8. In our everyday lives, what difference does it make that we can know that our inheritance is certain?

9. When have you been most prone to question your salvation?

10. How has the Holy Spirit reassured you in times of doubt?

Thank God that he keeps his promises and that he has sent his Spirit to live within you. Pray for the continual assurance that in Christ your inheritance is sure.

Now or Later

- Find examples of guarantees. Notice any "fine print" or conditions that allow the guarantor to go back on the promise. Compare conditional human guarantees with the guarantee of the Holy Spirit.
- Study 2 Corinthians 1:21-22; 5:1-5, in which Paul speaks of the Holy Spirit as the deposit and guarantee of "what is to come."

Suggested hymns to read or sing
Seal Us, Holy Spirit
Gracious Spirit, Dwell with Me
Spirit of the Living God, Fall Afresh on Me

5

Counselor

"If you were me, what would *you* do?" We never ask that question casually. When we need advice, we seek out wise people whom we know we can trust. No one knowingly seeks counsel from an unwise person.

Bad advice is not difficult to find. It is available everywhere from all sorts of sources. Sometimes people pay good money for bad advice. Bad advice can be costly, not only financially but in time, health, relationships and peace of mind.

GROUP DISCUSSION. Complete these sentences:

The best advice I ever received was to _____
_____.

The name of the person who gave me that advice was_____
_____. I took the advice because
_____
_____.

PERSONAL REFLECTION. If two people give you conflicting advice, how do you decide which to follow?

Only hours before he was arrested in Gethsemane, Jesus met with his disciples in an upper room to celebrate the Passover. The disciples' mood turned somber when Jesus began to talk about leaving them and going to a place where they could not yet follow. But Jesus promised his followers a constant source of wise counsel. *Read John 14:15-27.*

---

1. Imagine that you are one of the disciples in the upper room. How do your emotions rise and fall as you hear Jesus say these words?

---

2. Notice the name for the Spirit in verse 17: "The Spirit of truth." What meaning and purpose does that title suggest to you?

---

3. Jesus said he would send "another Counselor" (v. 16). The one Jesus would send is the Greek word *parakletos,* variously translated *Counselor* (NIV and RSV), *helper* (TEV and NASB) and *comforter* (KJV). The word is literally *one called alongside.* Where do you most need someone to come alongside you, help you and give you guidance?

---

4. The Greek word for *another* (v. 16) means "another like himself" rather than "another of a different sort." How does that insight affect your understanding of the Holy Spirit?

5. How will believers' experience of the Spirit differ from that of the world (vv. 16-19)?

6. The disciples are frightened to think that Jesus is about to leave them. How would his words in verses 18-24 bring them comfort?

7. What will the Holy Spirit do for the disciples after Jesus goes (vv. 25-27)?

8. How has the Spirit worked as a counselor for you and guided your decisions?

9. Jesus left his disciples with his own peace (v. 27). How has the Spirit brought you peace in troubled times?

10. What are some questions or concerns for which you need the counsel of the Holy Spirit?

11. How will you pray specifically for the Spirit's guidance this week?

Thank the Lord that you can draw on the wisdom of the Holy Spirit. Ask the Spirit to guide you in every decision this coming week. Pray that you will know the peace of Christ in all circumstances.

Now or Later

- Find an object or a symbol to remind you of a particular issue for which you need the wisdom and counsel of the Holy Spirit. Or simply write your question on a card. Place it where it will remind you regularly to pray for the Spirit's guidance.

- Study 1 Peter 1:10-12 and 2 Peter 1:19-21 concerning the role of the Holy Spirit in the revelation of Scripture.

Suggested hymns to read or sing
Holy Spirit, Faithful Guide
Holy Spirit, Truth Divine
The Comforter Has Come (O Spread the Tidings 'Round)

6

Advocate

Romans 8:26-27

Our hometown newspaper is called the *Advocate*, pronounced to rhyme with fate. Regardless of how you pronounce the word, an *advocate* is someone who stands up for others, especially for those with limited power or voice in society. A person may serve as an advocate for victims of crime or for people with disabilities or for children with learning problems. An advocate is a defender who pleads the cause of those who cannot defend themselves.

In session 5, you saw that the Holy Spirit is the *parakletos*, the "one called alongside." Beside *counselor*, another meaning of the word is *advocate*. The Spirit speaks up for us when we are defenseless before God.

GROUP DISCUSSION. When has someone stood up for you or spoken up on your behalf? What was your relationship with that person before and afterward?

PERSONAL REFLECTION. If you could not speak or act for yourself, who would you want to speak and act on your behalf, and why?

The apostle Paul longed to visit the Christians in Rome but had not been able to do so. Still hoping to see them eventually, he wrote the church in Rome a lengthy letter in which he set forth his case for the Christian faith and gave many practical instructions for Christian living. *Read Romans 8:26-27.*

---

1. The phrase "in the same way," which introduces this passage (v. 26), refers to our hope for the redemption of our earthly bodies (vv. 22-25). What contrasts does Paul draw between believers and the Holy Spirit?

---

2. Paul writes that the Spirit helps us in our weakness (v. 26). The word *helps* in the Greek is the action of one who takes hold of the other side of a load and helps lift it. When have you sensed the Holy Spirit helping you carry a load you could not bear alone?

---

3. In what circumstances have you felt weakness or insufficiency in praying for others?

---

4. When have you felt weakness or insufficiency in praying for yourself?

5. According to this passage, what is the Holy Spirit's involvement in our prayers?

6. How does Paul convey the Spirit's exertion and earnestness in prayer for us (v. 26)?

7. How can we be sure that the Spirit's prayers are in line what with God wants (v. 27)?

8. How do you respond to the idea that the Holy Spirit intercedes for you?

9. How would you respond to someone who said, "I can pray for anything I want, because the Holy Spirit changes my words around so they fit what God wants, so my answer is guaranteed"?

10. What are some areas in which you are uncertain how to pray according to God's will?

---

11. What help or comfort do you draw from this Scripture passage concerning prayer?

Ask the Holy Spirit to pray for you, not to get out of doing your own praying, but because he has perfect knowledge of your mind and the mind of God.

Now or Later

Pray the following prayer, filling in the blank lines with as many different concerns as you wish, one at a time. Keep a reminder of this prayer so you can bring concerns to God throughout the week.

"Holy Spirit, I am not sure how to pray for _____, but I know that I want God's will to be done. You are the one who comes alongside us and pleads for us. I ask you to intercede with the Father on behalf of _____ according to the will of God."

Suggested hymns to read or sing
Prayer Is the Soul's Sincere Desire
Spirit of God, Descend Upon My Heart
Fill Me Now (Hover O'er Me, Holy Spirit)

7

Anointing Oil

1 John 2:20-27

We use olive oil for salad dressings and in Italian cooking, and we know it is supposed to be healthier than other oils. In the land of the Bible, where olive trees flourish, olive oil has long been a staple in food preparation. It also served as fuel for lamps.

In biblical times olive oil had another, more sacred use. Kings, priests and prophets were anointed with olive oil as a sign that they were singled out by God. The Greek word *Christos* (Hebrew *Messiah*) literally means "Anointed One." It is not surprising that Jesus Christ is the one who gives his followers the anointing of the Holy Spirit.

GROUP DISCUSSION. In what areas of life do you feel you need greater wisdom and insight? Why do you feel you lack wisdom or insight in those areas?

PERSONAL REFLECTION. When have you felt that the Holy Spirit gave you special insight into a situation? How did you know it was the Spirit?

In the letter we call 1 John, the apostle John wrote to Christians who were being influenced by false teachers. He reminded them of the certainty of what they had been taught, and he reassured them that they did not need any exotic new teachings to supplement their knowledge of Christ. *Read 1 John 2:20-27.*

---

1. The noun *anointing* appears four times in this passage (vv. 20, 27). In each occurrence what do you learn about this anointing?

---

2. The Holy One (v. 20) is a name given to Christ in the Gospels and the book of Acts. Verses 21-23 refer to a specific lie that will be countered by the Holy One's anointing. What examples of the same falsehood do you encounter today?

---

3. Suppose you are in the church to whom John is writing. Some very persuasive and seemingly knowledgeable people in the church are teaching something different from your understanding of Christ. How would John's letter affect you?

4. Why might believers be tempted to leave the truth of the gospel, which they heard "from the beginning" (vv. 24-25)?

5. Christians routinely accept teaching from pastors, Sunday school teachers and Bible study leaders—just as you are doing right now! John himself wrote this letter to instruct believers. How would you explain his statement that "you do not need anyone to teach you" (vv. 26-27)?

At the Last Supper with John and the other disciples, Jesus makes a promise to them and to all his followers. *Read John 16:12-14.*

6. At this point Jesus' disciples are distressed and confused by his talk of going away. What hope would they gain from his promise?

7. Comparing the work of the promised Holy Spirit with the *anointing* of 1 John 2:20-27, what do you learn about the identity of the anointing?

8. In both the John and 1 John passages, how will the Spirit honor Christ?

9. Although the Holy Spirit's guidance is available to every Christian, we can choose to defy or ignore it. What are some consequences of acting against the Spirit's guidance?

10. In what circumstances have you recently experienced the Spirit's guidance?

11. What is an impending decision for which you need to be led by the Spirit?

Pray for sensitivity to the guidance of the Holy Spirit and for courage to obey.

Now or Later

- Study Luke 4:14-30, in which Jesus visits the synagogue at Nazareth and proclaims that he is the One anointed by the Spirit of the Lord.
- Expand your study of Jesus' promise of the Holy Spirit by studying John 14:15-30 and 15:26—16:16.

Suggested hymns to read or sing
Hail to the Lord's Anointed
Love Divine, All Loves Excelling

8

Giver of Gifts

1 Corinthians 12:1-11

When concert or theater programs list the names of donors, there are always gifts from "Anonymous." The giver does not wish to be known. Anonymity does not bother us on a concert program, but when we receive a beautiful gift, we do not want the tag to say "From Anonymous." We want a name, not only to satisfy our curiosity but so we can thank the giver.

Gifts of abilities for ministry never say "From Anonymous." They are all given by the Holy Spirit as he chooses. We can never exercise our gifts with pride but only with humility and gratitude.

GROUP DISCUSSION. When have you received a gift that was meant to benefit someone else more than you? How did you react to receiving it?

PERSONAL REFLECTION. When you give a gift, do you tend to choose something useful or something of beauty? Have you ever achieved both in one gift?

The apostle Paul spent several years preaching and teaching in Corinth, a cosmopolitan city known as a center of pagan worship and immorality. Paul supported himself by working as a tentmaker with Priscilla and Aquila. Later he wrote several letters to the Christians in Corinth, who were experiencing internal conflict and disunity. *Read 1 Corinthians 12:1-11.*

1. Throughout this passage what are the various actions of the Holy Spirit?

2. Who have you known that seemed to have a gift from the Holy Spirit to minister in a particular way? Describe that person and gift.

3. The Corinthian Christians had once been pagans who worshiped idols (v. 2). What guidance does Paul offer to distinguish between their previous spiritual activities and the genuine work of the Holy Spirit (vv. 1-3)?

4. In verses 4-7, how does Paul deal with the problem of disunity?

5. Consider the various spiritual gifts Paul mentions (vv. 8-10). How does each give evidence of the Holy Spirit working in the life of the church?

6. In verse 11, Paul emphasizes the same point he made in verses 4-6, that all gifts for ministry are given by the same Holy Spirit. Why do you think he makes the point again?

7. When and how have you experienced Christian unity in a fellowship of believers with diverse spiritual gifts?

8. Some Christians tend to elevate certain gifts of the Spirit over the other gifts. How does such an attitude disrupt what the Spirit wants to accomplish "for the common good" (v. 7)?

9. Do you think that you tend to elevate one spiritual gift over the others? If you do, which one, and why?

10. How have others discerned gifts of the Holy Spirit in your life?

11. How have you been blessed by other people's gifts of the Holy Spirit? Think of two or three that particularly stand out.

12. How will you express gratitude both to the Holy Spirit and to one or more of those people for how they have influenced your life?

Thank God for the gifts of the Spirit working through others. Thank him also for blessing others through your own spiritual gifts. Pray for more openness to recognize the gifts the Spirit has given you.

Now or Later

- Study Paul's other enumerations of spiritual gifts in Romans 12:1-8 and Ephesians 4:1-13.
- Write a letter of appreciation to someone whose spiritual gift of ministry has made a significant difference in your life.

Suggested hymns to read or sing
There's a Sweet, Sweet Spirit in this Place
Where the Spirit of the Lord Is

Leader's Notes

MY GRACE IS SUFFICIENT FOR YOU. (2 COR 12:9)

Leading a Bible discussion can be an enjoyable and rewarding experience. But it can also be *scary*—especially if you've never done it before. If this is your feeling, you're in good company. When God asked Moses to lead the Israelites out of Egypt, he replied, "O LORD, please send someone else to do it" (Ex 4:13). It was the same with Solomon, Jeremiah and Timothy, but God helped these people in spite of their weaknesses, and he will help you as well.

You don't need to be an expert on the Bible or a trained teacher to lead a Bible discussion. The idea behind these inductive studies is that the leader guides group members to discover for themselves what the Bible has to say. This method of learning will allow group members to remember much more of what is said than a lecture would.

These studies are designed to be led easily. As a matter of fact, the flow of questions through the passage from observation to interpretation to application is so natural that you may feel that the studies lead themselves. This study guide is also flexible. You can use it with a variety of groups—student, professional, neighborhood or church groups. Each study takes forty-five to sixty minutes in a group setting.

There are some important facts to know about group dynamics and encouraging discussion. The suggestions listed below should enable you to effectively and enjoyably fulfill your role as leader.

Preparing for the Study

1. Ask God to help you understand and apply the passage in your own life. Unless this happens, you will not be prepared to lead others.

Pray too for the various members of the group. Ask God to open your hearts to the message of his Word and motivate you to action.

2. Read the introduction to the entire guide to get an overview of the entire book and the issues which will be explored.

3. As you begin each study, read and reread the assigned Bible passage to familiarize yourself with it.

4. This study guide is based on the New International Version of the Bible. It will help you and the group if you use this translation as the basis for your study and discussion.

5. Carefully work through each question in the study. Spend time in meditation and reflection as you consider how to respond.

6. Write your thoughts and responses in the space provided in the study guide. This will help you to express your understanding of the passage clearly.

7. It might help to have a Bible dictionary handy. Use it to look up any unfamiliar words, names or places. (For additional help on how to study a passage, see chapter five of *How to Lead a LifeGuide Bible Study,* InterVarsity Press.)

8. Consider how you can apply the Scripture to your life. Remember that the group will follow your lead in responding to the studies. They will not go any deeper than you do.

9. Once you have finished your own study of the passage, familiarize yourself with the leader's notes for the study you are leading. These are designed to help you in several ways. First, they tell you the purpose the study guide author had in mind when writing the study. Take time to think through how the study questions work together to accomplish that purpose. Second, the notes provide you with additional background information or suggestions on group dynamics for various questions. This information can be useful when people have difficulty understanding or answering a question. Third, the leader's notes can alert you to potential problems you may encounter during the study.

10. If you wish to remind yourself of anything mentioned in the leader's notes, make a note to yourself below that question in the study.

Leading the Study

1. Begin the study on time. Open with prayer, asking God to help the group to understand and apply the passage.

2. Be sure that everyone in your group has a study guide. Encourage the group to prepare beforehand for each discussion by reading the introduction to the guide and by working through the questions in the study.

3. At the beginning of your first time together, explain that these studies are meant to be discussions, not lectures. Encourage the members of the group to participate. However, do not put pressure on those who may be hesitant to speak during the first few sessions. You may want to suggest the following guidelines to your group.

☐ Stick to the topic being discussed.

☐ Your responses should be based on the verses which are the focus of the discussion and not on outside authorities such as commentaries or speakers.

☐ These studies focus on a particular passage of Scripture. Only rarely should you refer to other portions of the Bible. This allows for everyone to participate in in-depth study on equal ground.

☐ Anything said in the group is considered confidential and will not be discussed outside the group unless specific permission is given to do so.

☐ We will listen attentively to each other and provide time for each person present to talk.

☐ We will pray for each other.

4. Have a group member read the introduction at the beginning of the discussion.

5. Every session begins with a group discussion question. The question or activity is meant to be used before the passage is read. The question introduces the theme of the study and encourages group members to begin to open up. Encourage as many members as possible to participate, and be ready to get the discussion going with your own response.

This section is designed to reveal where our thoughts or feelings need to be transformed by Scripture. That is why it is especially important not to read the passage before the discussion question is asked. The passage will tend to color the honest reactions people would otherwise give because they are, of course, supposed to think the way the Bible does.

You may want to supplement the group discussion question with an icebreaker to help people to get comfortable. See the community section of *Small Group Idea Book* for more ideas.

You also might want to use the personal reflection question with your group. Either allow a time of silence for people to respond individually or discuss it together.

6. Have a group member (or members if the passage is long) read aloud the passage to be studied. Then give people several minutes to read the passage again silently so that they can take it all in.

7. Question 1 will generally be an overview question designed to briefly survey the passage. Encourage the group to look at the whole passage, but try to avoid getting sidetracked by questions or issues that will be addressed later in the study.

8. As you ask the questions, keep in mind that they are designed to be used just as they are written. You may simply read them aloud. Or you may prefer to express them in your own words.

There may be times when it is appropriate to deviate from the study guide. For example, a question may have already been answered. If so, move on to the next question. Or someone may raise an important question not covered in the guide. Take time to discuss it, but try to keep the group from going off on tangents.

9. Avoid answering your own questions. If necessary, repeat or rephrase them until they are clearly understood. Or point out something you read in the leader's notes to clarify the context or meaning. An eager group quickly becomes passive and silent if they think the leader will do most of the talking.

10. Don't be afraid of silence. People may need time to think about the question before formulating their answers.

11. Don't be content with just one answer. Ask, "What do the rest of you think?" or "Anything else?" until several people have given answers to the question.

12. Acknowledge all contributions. Try to be affirming whenever possible. Never reject an answer. If it is clearly off-base, ask, "Which

verse led you to that conclusion?" or again, "What do the rest of you think?"

13. Don't expect every answer to be addressed to you, even though this will probably happen at first. As group members become more at ease, they will begin to truly interact with each other. This is one sign of healthy discussion.

14. Don't be afraid of controversy. It can be very stimulating. If you don't resolve an issue completely, don't be frustrated. Move on and keep it in mind for later. A subsequent study may solve the problem.

15. Periodically summarize what the group has said about the passage. This helps to draw together the various ideas mentioned and gives continuity to the study. But don't preach.

16. At the end of the Bible discussion you may want to allow group members a time of quiet to work on an idea under "Now or Later." Then discuss what you experienced. Or you may want to encourage group members to work on these ideas between meetings. Give an opportunity during the session for people to talk about what they are learning.

17. Conclude your time together with conversational prayer, adapting the prayer suggestion at the end of the study to your group. Ask for God's help in following through on the commitments you've made.

18. End on time.

Many more suggestions and helps are found in *How to Lead a LifeGuide Bible Study*.

Components of Small Groups
A healthy small group should do more than study the Bible. There are four components to consider as you structure your time together.

Nurture. Small groups help us to grow in our knowledge and love of God. Bible study is the key to making this happen and is the foundation of your small group.

Community. Small groups are a great place to develop deep friendships with other Christians. Allow time for informal interaction before and after each study. Plan activities and games that will help you get to know each other. Spend time having fun together—going on a picnic or cooking dinner together.

Worship and prayer. Your study will be enhanced by spending time praising God together in prayer or song. Pray for each other's needs—and keep track of how God is answering prayer in your group. Ask God to help you to apply what you are learning in your study.

Outreach. Reaching out to others can be a practical way of applying what you are learning, and it will keep your group from becoming self-focused. Host a series of evangelistic discussions for your friends or neighbors. Clean up the yard of an elderly friend. Serve at a soup kitchen together, or spend a day working on a Habitat house.

Many more suggestions and helps in each of these areas are found in *Small Group Idea Book*. Information on building a small group can be found in *Small Group Leaders' Handbook* and *The Big Book on Small Groups* (both from InterVarsity Press). Reading through one of these books would be worth your time.

Study 1. Wind/Breath. Ezekiel 37:1-14.

Purpose: To find hope in the Holy Spirit's life-giving power.

Question 1. "The root meaning [of both the Hebrew and Greek words] is 'a movement of air,' 'breeze,' or 'wind,' and so 'breath.' By extension it became the life principle" (S. V. McCasland, "Spirit," in *Interpreter's Dictionary of the Bible,* vol. 4, ed. George A. Buttrick [Nashville: Abingdon, 1962], p. 434).

Question 3. "The large amount of bones described here implies that this was the scene of a major catastrophe. The depiction of a large number of corpses that had been denied a proper burial is reminiscent of many battle scenes and descriptions of battle scenes found in the earliest periods of Mesopotamian and Egyptian history" (John H. Walton, Victor H. Matthews and Mark W. Chavalas, eds., *The IVP Bible Background Commentary: Old Testament* [Downers Grove, Ill.: InterVarsity Press, 1998], p. 722).

Question 6. "When Ezekiel prophetically announces the word of the 'Sovereign LORD' in the valley of dry bones, he announces God's comprehensive power over death and life, the very *breath* (the Hebrew word can also mean *wind*) of life: 'Come from the four winds, O breath, and breathe into these slain, that they may live' (Ezek

37:9)" (Leland Ryken, James C. Wilhoit and Tremper Longman III, eds., *Dictionary of Biblical Imagery* [Downers Grove, Ill.: InterVarsity Press, 1998], p. 952).

Question 7. "After the fall of Jerusalem the people would have been scattered and dispirited. The oracle had a simple message: that the dead nation of Israel would one day be revived and return to their own land. The dry bones became living warriors. An equally powerful transformation would one day be applied to Israel. The force of this vision has brought hope to many down the centuries. The power of God can change even the most hopeless of lives and situations" (L. John McGregor, in *New Bible Commentary, 21st Century Edition*, ed. D. A. Carson et al. [Downers Grove, Ill.: InterVarsity Press, 1994], p. 740).

Question 9. You may want to allow a few moments of silence before you invite people to respond to this question. Then allow them to name areas of dryness if they are comfortable. After that, encourage them to hear God's invitation in these words.

Study 2. Water. John 4:1-14; 7:37-39.

Purpose: To continually draw on the Holy Spirit for spiritual needs.

Group discussion. Have a container of water or individual glasses ready for this question.

Question 1. "Apart from the environs of the Sea of Galilee and the Jordan River, and a few fertile plains, the Holy Land is dependent on springs, wells and cisterns. The frequent experience of thirst and the anticipation of water (Ps 42:1-2), the need to husband water resources, the labor of drawing and carrying water, the contrast of fresh and long-stored water—all these are recurrent features of biblical experience. . . . Since the drawing of well water was a laborious task usually reserved for women, we are not surprised to learn that the Samaritan woman whom Jesus meets at Jacob's well . . . is responsive to Jesus' offer of a living water that carries the promise of being miraculously replenished" (*Dictionary of Biblical Imagery*, p. 930).

"The site of Jacob's well is still known; it is within view of Mount Gerizim, which was holy to the Samaritans" (Craig S. Keener, *The IVP Bible Background Commentary: New Testament* [Downers Grove, Ill.: InterVarsity Press, 1993], p. 272).

Question 3. "The idea of *drink* for physical needs led naturally into the comment about *the gift of God* (10), which turned it into a spiritual issue. The woman was thinking of Jesus as a typical Jew, but Jesus took her up on this. If she had known his identity she would have asked for *living water*. This expression had a double meaning, either running water, *i.e.* spring water, or spiritual water, *i.e.* connected with the Spirit" (*New Bible Commentary,* p. 1033).

Question 8. "The 'last day' of the Feast of Tabernacles (7:2) probably refers to the eighth day. For at least the first seven days of the feast, priests marched in procession from the Pool of Siloam to the temple and poured out water at the base of the altar. Pilgrims to the feast watched this ritual, which Jews throughout the Roman world thus knew; it was even commemorated on souvenir jars they could take home with them.

"The public reading of Scripture at this feast included the one passage in the Prophets that emphasized this feast, Zechariah 14, which was interpreted in conjunction with Ezekiel 47. Together these texts taught that rivers of living water would flow forth from the temple (in Jewish teaching, at the very center of the earth, from the foundation stone of the temple), bringing life to all the earth. The water-drawing ceremony . . . pointed toward this hope" (*IVP Bible Background Commentary: NT,* p. 283).

Question 10. "[In the Gospel of John] water is a frequent metaphor for the Spirit (see 7:39). It symbolizes the spiritual renewal promised in the Old Testament prophets and offered in Christ. This living water is flowing within Christ (7:37-39) who becomes a renewing spring from whom we are invited to drink (4:13-14). . . . He is the fountain from which the Holy Spirit may be obtained" (G. M. Burge, "Water," in *Dictionary of Jesus and the Gospels,* ed. Joel B. Green, Scot McKnight and I. Howard Marshall [Downers Grove, Ill.: InterVarsity Press, 1992], p. 870).

"Jesus announces that anyone who is truly thirsty should come to him and drink (Jn 7:37). Moreover, believers in Jesus will find that rivers of living water will flow out of their own heart (Jn 7:38). This water, the writer is careful to explain, is the promised Holy Spirit" (*Dictionary of Biblical Imagery,* p. 931).

Study 3. Fire. Acts 2:1-4, 14-18.
Purpose: To discover varied ways the Spirit works as a fire in our lives.
Group discussion. If you can, meet in a place where there is a fire-place—or meet around a campfire or fire pit. Use these questions: What is this fire doing for us right now? What would you miss most if this fire were extinguished right now?
Background. "The *day of Pentecost* was a major festival in the Jewish religion, also known as the Feast of Weeks. The holiday celebrated the wheat harvest, and in some Jewish traditions was also associated with the giving of the law and the renewal of the covenant. Jerusalem was crowded with Jewish visitors from abroad (see 2:5). Some of these were about to celebrate a new kind of harvest and covenant renewal! The words for *wind* and 'spirit' are the same in Greek (as they are in Hebrew), the two concepts are so closely identified (*cf.* Jn. 3:8). On Mt Sinai (Ex. 19:18), the fire on the mountain represented the presence of God there, perhaps the *tongues of fire* here are similarly representing that presence for the disciples *were filled with the Holy Spirit*" (*New Bible Commentary,* p. 1071).

The Scripture does not say precisely whether the Holy Spirit came only upon the apostles or upon the 120 believers who regularly met together (Acts 1:14-15). "They" (2:1) could be the same "they" as 1:26, the apostles. If it refers to "the believers" of 1:15, they had obviously moved from their place of prayer (1:13) to a more public place, since their behavior quickly attracted a large crowd (2:5-6).

Question 2. Although there was a violent wind, the flames did not spread wildly through the house, but divided into separate flames, which rested on each person. Even if there was only the sound of wind (v. 2), natural flames would have burned them. Their clothing or hair did not catch fire; rather they became filled with the Holy Spirit. The miraculous event reminds us of God's appearance to Moses in the burning bush; "though the bush was on fire it did not burn up" (Ex 3:2).

Question 3. The fire appeared in the shape of tongues, and the apostles began to speak in other tongues.

"Like the image of wind, the tongues of fire suggest a divine power invading the gathered community in Jerusalem. The image of the

Spirit as fire is also evoked in a setting where spiritual gifts are being exercised in the midst of the worshiping community at Thessalonica. Paul, in addressing the 'testing' of prophecy, instructs the Thessalonians that they must not 'quench' the Spirit (1 Thess 5:19). The true activity of the Spirit is subject to discernment, but where it is truly present it should not be snuffed out like a lamp light or a fire" (*Dictionary of Biblical Imagery*, p. 393).

Question 4. "That God should appear as fire is appropriate for many reasons. Just as all physical life depends on the fire that is the sun (cf. Rev 16:8), so does all spiritual life depend on God. Just as fire both purifies and destroys, so does God purify the righteous and destroy the wicked ('for our God is a consuming fire,' Heb 12:29 RSV). Just as fire lights up the blackness of night, so does God overcome the dark powers of evil. Just as fire is mysterious and immaterial, so too is God enigmatic and incorporeal. And just as fire is always flickering and changing its shape and cannot be held for examination, so is God always the indefinable who is beyond our grasp" (*Dictionary of Biblical Imagery*, p. 287).

Study 4. Pledge. Ephesians 1:11-14.

Purpose: To draw reassurance from God's pledge of the Holy Spirit within us.

Question 3. Ephesus was the site of a great temple to the goddess Artemis. Though she shared the name of the Greek goddess of the hunt (Diana to the Romans), she was a very different goddess. "The Ephesian Artemis was not a virgin huntress, but a fecund mother; not a moon-goddess, but a goddess of fertility in man and beast and vegetation. . . . Her worship was not confined to Ephesus, but was practiced in nearly all the cities of Asia, in many places on the Greek mainland, in the S of Gaul, in Syria, and in Rome itself; so that there is no exaggeration in the description of her magnificence as one 'whom all Asia and the world worship' (Acts 19:27)" (F. W. Beare, "Artemis," in *Interpreter's Dictionary of the Bible,* vol. 1, ed. George A. Buttrick [Nashville: Abingdon, 1962], p. 242).

Question 5. According to denominational and theological perspectives, people may interpret what it means to be chosen and predestined in this context in different ways. Don't get sidetracked by this. Predestination could be a topic for another session.

Questions 6-7. "The Holy Spirit is also the *arrabōn*, a first install-ment, deposit, pledge or a down payment. In a marketplace transac-tion it represents the portion of the purchase price paid in advance, a payment that guarantees future payment of the whole. In 2 Corin-thians 1:22 Paul speaks of the Spirit as the down payment, or 'guaran-tee' (RSV), that God's promises will be true. This guarantee is also a 'seal' *(sphragis sphragizomai),* implying God's mark of ownership. . . . In Ephesians 1:14 the Spirit is God's down payment on the believer's future, an interim gift, a prelude and foretaste of the inheritance that is to come" (*Dictionary of Biblical Imagery,* pp. 392-93).

Study 5. Counselor. John 14:15-27.

Purpose: To rely on the Spirit for wisdom in every decision.

Question 3. "The Spirit's coming, and being sent by our Lord from the Father, to testify of him, are personal characters, and plainly dis-tinguish him from the Father and the Son; and his title as the Spirit of truth, together with his proceeding from the Father, can agree to none but a Divine person. And that he proceeds from the Son, as well as from the Father, may be fairly argued from his being called the Spirit of Christ, 1 Peter 1:11; and from his being here said to be sent by Christ from the Father, as well as sent by the Father in his name" (John Wesley, *Notes on the Whole Bible: New Testament* [Albany, Ore.: Sage Digital Library, 1996], pp. 309-10).

Question 5. When the Gospel of John refers to the *world,* the Greek word is *kosmos,* which carries a meaning beyond the physical world and its inhabitants. *Kosmos* signifies "the system of this world set against God."

"It is . . . an axiom of the Bible that this world of human beings, the climax of the divine creation, the world that God made especially to reflect his glory, is now in rebellion against him. Through the trans-gression of one man, sin has entered into it (Rom. 5:18) with univer-sal consequences. It has become, as a result, a *disordered* world in the grip of the evil one (1 Jn. 5:19). And so, very frequently in the New Testament, and particularly in the Johannine writings, the word *kos-*

mos has a sinister significance. It is not the world as God intended it to be, but '*this* world' set over against God, following its own wisdom and living by the light of its own reason (1 Cor. 1:21), not recognizing the Source of all true life and illumination (Jn. 1:10)" (R. V. G. Tasker, "World," in *New Bible Dictionary*, 3rd ed., ed. D. R. W. Wood [Downers Grove, Ill.: InterVarsity Press, 1996], p. 1249).

Question 7. "The disciples cannot take in (16:12) or understand the significance of what Jesus has said and done until he is glorified (16:25). Consequently, the Spirit-Paraclete is given to *remind* them of Jesus' teaching (14:26) and to *interpret* it to them (e.g., 2:22). The main task of the Spirit in John is to provide a particular sort of charismatic wisdom: to bring true comprehension of the significance of the historical revelation in Christ" (*Dictionary of Jesus and the Gospels*, p. 350).

Study 6. Advocate. Romans 8:26-27.

Purpose: To trust the Holy Spirit to pray for us when we do not know what or how to pray.

Question 2. In the New Testament this Greek word for *helps* occurs only in Romans 8:26 and in Luke 10:40, where Martha asks Jesus to tell Mary to *help* her with household tasks.

The word "signifies to take hold with at the side for assistance . . . hence, to take a share in, help in bearing, to help in general" (W. E. Vine, *Expository Dictionary of New Testament Words,* vol. 2 [London: Oliphants, 1940], p. 214).

"The metaphor is of a helper supporting the weight in co-operation with the bearer and at the opposite end of the burden" (G. T. Thomson and F. Davidson, *The New Bible Commentary,* ed. Francis Davidson [Grand Rapids: Eerdmans, 1965], p. 954).

Questions 3-4. "There are two very obvious reasons why we cannot pray as we ought. First, we cannot pray aright because we cannot foresee the future. We cannot see a year or even an hour ahead; and we may well pray, therefore, to be saved from things which are for our good and we may well pray for things which would be to our ultimate harm. Second, we cannot pray aright because in any given situation we do not know what is best for us. We are often in the position of a child who wants something which would be bound only to hurt him; and God is often in the position of a parent who has to refuse his child's request or compel him to do something he does not want to do, because he knows what is to the child's good far better than the child himself" (William Barclay, *The Letter to the Romans,* rev. ed., Daily Bible Study Series [Philadelphia: Westminster Press, 1975], pp. 111-12).

Question 5. "Three persons are involved in our praying. First, we ourselves in our weakness do not know what to pray for. Secondly, the indwelling Spirit helps us by interceding for us and through us, with speechless groans but according to God's will. Thirdly, God the Father, who both searches our hearts and knows the Spirit's mind, hears and answers accordingly. Of these actors, however, it is the Spirit who is emphasized. Paul makes three statements about him. First, 'the Spirit helps us' (because of our weakly, half-saved situation); secondly, 'the Spirit intercedes for us' (because of our ignorance of what to pray for); and thirdly, 'the Spirit intercedes according to God's will' (and therefore God listens and responds)" (John Stott, *Romans: God's Good News for the World* [Downers Grove, Ill.: Inter-Varsity Press, 1994], pp. 245-46).

Question 6. "[The Spirit] is our perfect advocate before a holy God; he intercedes or speaks for us with 'groans that words cannot express . . . in accordance with God's will' (Rom 8:26, 27 NIV). The Holy Spirit's role as 'Advocate' or 'Paraclete' . . . of the believer combines the work of a friend who also frankly tells you what is wrong (it can mean prosecuting counsel, defending counsel or friend), but only so that, once it is exposed, it can be put right. There is nothing enigmatic about the image of a Paraclete. It is part of the Paraclete's comfort and encouragement to dispel illusion but to love us still" (*Dictionary of Biblical Imagery,* p. 391).

"It is truly amazing that, having written of the groaning creation and of the groaning church [vv. 22-23], Paul should now write of the groaning Spirit. Indeed, some commentators have resisted this, declaring that the Spirit never groans, and that Paul means only that he causes us to groan. Yet Paul's language is clear. The Spirit intercedes for us in unspoken groanings. That is, his intercession is accompanied by them and expressed in them. True, God's creation and God's children groan because of their present state of imperfection, and there is nothing imperfect about the Holy Spirit. It must be, therefore, that the Holy Spirit identifies with our groans, with the pain of the world and the church, and shares in the longing for the final freedom of both. We and he groan together" (Stott, *Romans,* p. 245).

Study 7. Anointing Oil. 1 John 2:20-27.

Purpose: To gain confidence that we have the Holy Spirit as our guide and teacher.

Question 1. The *anointing* is from the Holy One (a name given to Christ in the Gospels and the book of Acts) and it enlightens believers with the truth (v. 20). The anointing remains in believers, is sufficient for teaching and is authentic (v. 27).

Concerning anointing with oil: "Perhaps the most frequent use of oil mentioned in the Bible is that of anointing. Most familiar is the custom of anointing a king (1 Sam. 10:1; 16:1, 13; 2 Kings 9:3, 6; 11:12), a priest (Lev. 8:30), or a prophet (Isa. 61:1). Since this anointing oil was called 'oil of gladness' (Ps. 45:7) . . . it may be assumed that it was a joyous occasion" (J. F. Ross, "Oil," in *Interpreter's Dictionary of the Bible,* vol. 3, ed. George A. Buttrick [Nashville: Abingdon, 1962], p. 592).

Question 2. The specific lie is the denial that Jesus is the Christ, the Son of God. This falsehood is the basis for any concept of Jesus as *only* a great human teacher, liberator or example.

Question 4. "'What you have heard from the beginning' is the apostolic witness to Christ (1 Jn 1:1-3), which in the Gospel of John became Scripture. Those anointed are not the false teachers who have rejected this apostolic witness and have left the orthodox Christian community, but precisely those who have accepted the witness, in which it remains" (Walter C. Kaiser Jr., Peter H. Davids, F. F. Bruce and Manfred T. Brauch, eds., *Hard Sayings of the Bible* [Downers Grove, Ill.: InterVarsity Press, 1996], p. 735).

Question 5. "John has at least three reasons for writing this. First, the false teachers were probably claiming to have some secret knowledge into which they had been initiated and which the orthodox Christians did not have. Nonsense, says John, you yourself have the real, not the counterfeit. Unlike them you have Truth himself within.

"Second, these people already have received the apostolic witness and remain in it, the anointing of the Spirit showing them that it is indeed true. . . . Third, the Spirit within will guide them into truth. While teachers may be helpful and an exhortation or teaching like 1 John useful, John trusts that the Spirit himself will be the real teacher, showing them the true and exposing the false" (*Hard Sayings*, p. 735).

"John reminds the church that each member has been equally anointed with the Spirit. . . . Spiritual discernment is the task of every person. To be a Christian is to possess the Spirit, and no one may come along claiming exclusive spiritual insight. . . . Christians must be well-grounded and confident in the authenticity of their own spiritual experience and not swayed by the seemingly more compelling experiences of others" (G. M. Burge, "Letters of John," in *Dictionary of the Later New Testament & Its Developments*, ed. Ralph P. Martin and Peter H. Davids [Downers Grove, Ill.: InterVarsity Press, 1997], p. 593).

Question 7. In both Scripture passages the Holy Spirit is sent by Christ, remains with believers and guides believers into truth.

"Christians have an indwelling Instructor, the Holy Spirit. . . . Doubt as to the availability of guidance would be a slur on the faithfulness of the Holy Spirit to his ministry. . . . It is impossible to doubt that guidance is a reality intended for, and promised to, every child of God" (J. I. Packer, *Knowing God* [Downers Grove, Ill.: InterVarsity Press, 1973], p. 234).

Question 8. The Spirit will bring glory to Christ by making him known (Jn 16:14-15) and will verify that Jesus is the Christ (1 Jn 2:20-23).

Study 8. Giver of Gifts. 1 Corinthians 12:1-11.
Purpose: To appreciate that Christians' diverse gifts for ministry all come from one Holy Spirit.

Question 1. "The term 'spiritual gifts' represents the common rendering in English of the Greek neuter plural noun *charismata*, formed from *charizesthai* (to show favor, give freely), which is related to the noun *charis* (grace); they are the concrete expression of *charis*, grace coming to visible effect in word or deed. . . . The lists of *charismata* in the New Testament (Rom. 12:6-8; 1 Cor. 12:4-11, 28-30; *cf.* Eph. 4:7-12) are clearly incomplete. Various classifications of the gifts have been attempted, but they fall most simply into two main categories—those which qualify their possessors for the ministry of the word and those which equip them for practical service. . . . Some gifts, such as those of apostleship, prophecy and teaching, were exercised in regular ministry; other gifts like tongues and healing were manifested occasionally. In some instances the gifts appear to involve a release or enhancement of natural ability, for example, the gifts of teaching, helping or leadership; others are clearly a special endowment: faith, gifts of healing and the power to work miracles" (W. G. Putman, "Spiritual Gifts," in *New Bible Dictionary,* 3rd ed., ed. D. R. W. Wood [Downers Grove, Ill.: InterVarsity Press, 1996], pp. 1130-31).

"The word *charisma* is a distinctively Pauline word (found elsewhere in the New Testament only in 1 Pet 4:10 and otherwise rarely in Greek literature at all). On its own the word has nothing to do with the Spirit; it picks up Spirit overtones only by context or by clear qualifiers. The noun has been formed from *charis* ('grace'), referring to *a concrete expression of grace*, which is what it means in its every instance in Paul. Thus in nearly half of its uses *charisma* designates a variety of ways God's grace has been evidenced among his people. It includes such diverse 'gifts' as eternal life (Rom 6:23; cf. Rom 5:15, 16), the special privileges granted to Israel (Rom 11:29, referring to Rom 9:4-5), celibacy and marriage (1 Cor 7:7) and deliverance from a deadly peril (2 Cor 1:11)" (Gordon D. Fee, "Gifts of the Spirit," in *Dictionary of Paul and His Letters,* ed. Gerald F. Hawthorne and Ralph P. Martin [Downers Grove, Ill.: InterVarsity Press, 1993], p. 340).

Question 3. "Paul indicates that prophesying is not necessarily a sign of godliness; pagans prophesied, too, and at Greek oracular shrines possessed persons prophesied ecstatically, inspired by gods other than the Christian God. Although interest in oracles had declined in this period, oracles and other forms of divination remained a strong influence on pagan culture. Paul can thus point to his readers' former behavior in paganism as a warning that ecstatic activity *by itself* cannot constitute proof that they are obeying God. (Verse 3 probably hypothetically contrasts two extreme examples of evil and true utterances)" (*IVP Bible Background Commentary: NT*, p. 478).

Question 5. Keep in mind that the subject of this study is the "*Giver of Gifts*," not the gifts themselves. Do not allow the group to get sidetracked into controversy over particular gifts such as healing or tongues. As much as possible, keep the discussion centered on the Holy Spirit as the One who bestows all ministry abilities.

Question 8. In churches today, as in Corinth, believers are tempted to exercise spiritual gifts as a way of displaying their own importance. "In secular Corinth the elite paraded their gifts and abilities believing that it was these that gave them status and significance. This false notion appears, in some cases, still to exist after conversion and in ministry" (Bruce Winter, in *New Bible Commentary, 21st Century Edition*, p. 1180).

Dale and Sandy Larsen are freelance writers living in Greenville, Illinois. Together they have written more than thirty books and Bible studies, including six other LifeGuide® Bible Studies and Jonathan Edwards, Teresa of Avila *and* Dietrich Bonhoeffer *in the Christian Classics Series.*

What Should We Study Next?

A good place to continue your study of Scripture would be with a book study. Many groups begin with a Gospel such as *Mark* (20 studies by Jim Hoover) or *John* (26 studies by Douglas Connelly). These guides are divided into two parts so that if twenty or twenty-six weeks seems like too much to do at once, the group can feel free to do half and take a break with another topic. Later you might want to come back to it. You might prefer to try a shorter letter. *Philippians* (9 studies by Donald Baker), *Ephesians* (11 studies by Andrew T. and Phyllis J. Le Peau) and *1 & 2 Timothy and Titus* (11 studies by Pete Sommer) are good options. If you want to vary your reading with an Old Testament book, consider *Ecclesiastes* (12 studies by Bill and Teresa Syrios) for a challenging and exciting study.

There are a number of interesting topical LifeGuide studies as well. Here are some options for filling three or four quarters of a year:

Basic Discipleship
Christian Beliefs, 12 studies by Stephen D. Eyre
Christian Character, 12 studies by Andrea Sterk & Peter Scazzero
Christian Disciplines, 12 studies by Andrea Sterk & Peter Scazzero
Evangelism, 12 studies by Rebecca Pippert & Ruth Siemens

Building Community
Fruit of the Spirit, 9 studies by Hazel Offner
Spiritual Gifts, 8 studies by R. Paul Stevens
Christian Community, 10 studies by Rob Suggs

Character Studies
David, 12 studies by Jack Kuhatschek
New Testament Characters, 10 studies by Carolyn Nystrom
Old Testament Characters, 12 studies by Peter Scazzero
Women of the Old Testament, 12 studies by Gladys Hunt

The Trinity
Meeting God, 12 studies by J. I. Packer
Meeting Jesus, 13 studies by Leighton Ford
Meeting the Spirit, 10 studies by Douglas Connelly

ALSO FOR SMALL GROUPS

Scripture Union produces a wide variety of resources for small groups. Among them are:

The Word made fresh! – a series of A4 discussion starters based on relevant contemporary teaching from internationally-known preacher Stephen Gaukroger; ten sessions with worksheets in each.

Connect Bible Studies – a range based on contemporary issues, looking at what biblical principles we might apply to understanding them.

Re:action series – food for thought on subjects that matter: icebreakers, opportunity for discussion and reflection, ideas for taking things further; seven sessions in each.

Essential 100 and *Essential Jesus* – 100 readings and notes in each, with group discussion questions at the end of each set of five. *Essential 100* gives a Bible overview; *Essential Jesus* gives the biblical panorama of the life and ministry of Jesus.

SU also has a free online magazine for small groups called **church@home**. Go to www.scriptureunion.org.uk/churchathome

SU publications are available from Christian bookshops, on the Internet, or via mail order. Advice on what would suit your group best is always available. You can:

- phone SU's mail order line: local rate number 08450 706006
- email info@scriptureunion.org.uk
- log on to www.scriptureunion.org.uk
- write to SU Mail Order, PO Box 5148, Milton Keynes MLO, MK2 2YX

Scripture Union
USING THE BIBLE TO INSPIRE CHILDREN, YOUNG PEOPLE AND ADULTS TO KNOW GOD